The  **CASSON
BECKMAN**

Guide to

DIRECTORS'
DUTIES AND
RESPONSIBILITIES

GW00832359

The CASSON BECKMAN Guide to DIRECTORS' DUTIES AND RESPONSIBILITIES

Your Questions Answered

Paul Ginman

KOGAN PAGE

CASSON BECKMAN
chartered accountants
& business advisers

Disclaimer

The masculine pronoun has been used throughout this book. This stems from a desire to avoid ugly and cumbersome language, and no discrimination, prejudice or bias is intended.

First published in 1992

Apart from any fair dealing for the purposes of research or private study, or criticism or review, as permitted under the Copyright, Designs and Patents Act, 1988, this publication may only be reproduced, stored or transmitted, in any form or by any means, with the prior permission in writing of the publishers, or in the case of reprographic reproduction in accordance with the terms of licences issued by the Copyright Licensing Agency. Enquiries concerning reproduction outside those terms should be sent to the publishers at the undermentioned address:

Kogan Page Limited
120 Pentonville Road
London N1 9JN

British Library Cataloguing in Publication Data

A CIP record for this book is available from the British Library.

ISBN 0 7494 0698 4

Typeset by DP Photosetting, Aylesbury, Bucks
Printed and bound in Great Britain by
Clays Ltd, St Ives plc

Contents

Foreword

One of the most important differences between being a director and a senior manager is that a director has duties and potential liabilities under the law. In the event of wrongdoing, the law does not recognise ignorance as an admissible defence. In running their companies to the best of their ability, directors are required to comply with their legal obligations. These apply to themselves, their companies, their employees, persons and companies with whom they trade, and society at large.

In the UK the Insolvency and Companies Acts have resulted in a substantial raising of the standards of skill and care expected of directors by the courts. Directors are now exposed to the possibility of disqualification, personal liability for the company's assets, liability for damages under civil law, or to criminal conviction in the event of failure by the company to comply with its legal obligations.

It is essential that anyone who accepts the position of director is fully aware of his obligations, and it is for this reason that the Institute of Directors, through its Centre for Director Development, operates a number of courses on the Role of the Company Director.

Mr Ginman's book provides an excellent introduction to the subject. He puts the concise questions every director should ask and then gently guides him through the answers. Armed with this information he will have a broad knowledge of his duties and responsibilities and will know better when to seek professional advice.

I recommend this guide as essential reading for all company directors.

Blenyth Jenkins
Director of Corporate Affairs, INSTITUTE OF DIRECTORS

About the author

Paul Ginman joined Mann Judd (which later merged with a 'big six' practice) in 1981, having completed a degree in accountancy at the University of Kent. In 1984 he joined Casson Beckman as the firm's first full-time technical manager, and became a partner in 1988. He is now responsible for the firm's technical division and for training in the general practice divisions.

Paul frequently lectures on directors' duties, and is involved in giving advice to directors on their position under companies legislation.

Preface

In producing this book we have attempted to set out the framework within which directors are expected to operate. We have adopted a question-and-answer format and have tried to simplify extremely complex and technical legislation. The downside of this approach is that sometimes generalisations have to be made. While we have tried to limit these, we would strongly recommend that professional advice be sought prior to commencing any particular course of action.

Paul Ginman FCA, 1992

Caveat

This book is intended only as a general guide to the scope of the law in question. It is not a complete statement of the law and should therefore not be acted or relied upon without further detailed advice. The law stated is based upon our understanding of the relevant legislation applicable to England and Wales in force at December 1991.

Acknowledgements

A book of this type is by its nature a team effort and I would like to thank, in particular, the following for their input into preparation of the text: John Tipping on taxation, Ian Holland and John Bennett on insolvency, and Timothy Webber on company law.

Introduction

A company is regarded in law as a separate legal entity, but it can operate and make decisions only through its board of directors and through its shareholders in general meeting. It is the board of directors that is responsible for the management of the company and for safeguarding its assets.

The role of a director should not be taken lightly. During recent years public expectation of directors' functions has increased greatly. Many new duties and corresponding personal liabilities have been created both by statute and through the courts. Failure to comply with legislation may result in civil or criminal liability, penalties being by way of a fine or imprisonment or both.

The Insolvency Act 1985 marked a major development in company law and in particular its application to corporate insolvencies. It also changed the rules relating to bankruptcy, but this is not covered in this book. The 1985 Act's provisions were consolidated along with the sections relating to insolvency from the Companies Act 1985 to produce the Insolvency Act 1986. Together with the Company Directors Disqualification Act 1986, the Act provided for the regulation and conduct of insolvencies and the management of companies prior to insolvency. It also reinforced existing fraudulent trading provisions and introduced a new civil offence of wrongful trading.

Directors are faced with important duties and responsibilities under these Acts, which apply to any persons occupying the position of director by whatever name they are called; ie, it is their role and duties and not their title which determines whether or not they are directors for the purposes of the Acts. The provisions also apply to any person in accordance with whose directions or instructions the directors of the company are accustomed to act, ie shadow directors.

The duties and responsibilities are extensive, and the aim of this book is to provide an outline of the major relevant areas. This should provide the basis for subsequent discussions with professional advisers.

This book is particularly aimed at persons considering a directorship, or newly appointed, although it should also act as a useful reminder to those who have held the post for some time.

1 The director's role

Who is a director?

There is no full definition of 'director' in law. The Companies Act 1985 states that the term 'director' includes any person occupying the position of director by whatever name called. Thus, directors are to be recognised by their functions and by the authority and power they exercise.

For certain taxation purposes, the term 'director' is given a specific definition. For instance, under the benefits-in-kind provisions, 'director' means:

- in relation to a company whose affairs are managed by a board of directors or similar body, a member of that board or similar body;

- in relation to a company whose affairs are managed by a single director or similar person, that director or person; and

- in relation to a company whose affairs are managed by the members themselves, a member of the company;

and includes any person in accordance with whose directions or instructions the directors of the company are accustomed to act. There is a proviso that a person giving advice as a professional will not be deemed to be a director just because the directors are accustomed to act on that advice.

How many directors should a company have?

Statute requires that every public company must have at least two directors. A private company is required to have at least one director who may not also act as the company secretary. There is no statutory maximum. It is generally considered unwise to have only one director because of the nature of the decisions which must be taken, which require a great deal of judgement, and problems which can arise as a result of illness etc. In addition to the minimum number of directors laid down by statute, the company's Articles of Association, which provide a constitutional framework within which the company operates, may increase the minimum or impose a maximum number of directors.

What is the company secretary's role?

Company secretaries are also officers of the company but are not, by virtue of their office, members of the board of directors. The duties of the company secretary will vary according to the size of company, but will always include arranging and convening meetings and maintaining statutory registers. A company secretary may also be appointed a director of the company.

What are the different types of directors?

The various types of directors are as follows:

1. An *executive director* is a person who, in addition to his position on the board, has managerial responsibilities for the day-to-day operations of the company.

2. A *non-executive director* is one who is invited onto the board to assist with policy and strategy decisions, but who does not work full-time for the company. The law makes no distinction between executive and non-executive directors. It is now considered good practice, irrespective of the size of the company, for all boards of directors to contain at least one non-executive director.

3. An *alternate director* is appointed by a director and is empowered to perform the duties of that director, usually at board meetings, in the temporary absence of the director appointing him. The power to appoint an

alternate director must be written into the company's Articles of Association, which should define precisely the rights, duties, and powers of an alternate director.

4. A *shadow director* is a person in accordance with whose directions or instructions the directors of the company are accustomed to act.

What are the implications of being a shadow director?

Shadow directors are subject to the same responsibilities and penalties as other directors regardless of the fact that they have not been formally appointed.

Is everyone who is called a director a director?

A person who is given the title of 'director', eg 'sales director', to give him status within the company, is not a director in company law, unless he is a member of the board of directors. It is essential that the exact status of these persons be made known to all who deal with the company. If the company represents any person as being a director, whether by intention or inference, and that person subsequently appears to exercise the authority of a director, the company will be unable to disclaim any transactions entered into on behalf of the company by that person, as an outsider is entitled to assume that the person is acting with the board's authority.

Is a director always an individual?

A company may also be a director. In this instance the company will appoint an individual as its representative to attend board meetings. The representative will be empowered to take decisions on behalf of the company, who is the director.

How are directors appointed?

Directors are generally elected by the shareholders in general meeting. Appointments are usually for a limited period as specified in the company's Articles of Association, after which the director becomes subject to re-election. The board of directors may normally fill any casual vacancy which arises or appoint additional directors up to the maximum permitted in the Articles of Association.

How are directors removed?

Directors may be removed by the shareholders in general meeting passing an ordinary resolution, ie one passed by a simple majority. A director may also resign at any time. It is important to note that the board of directors can strip a director of his executive duties, eg as managing director, but they cannot, under the Companies Acts, remove a director from office.

There are various other ways in which a director vacates his office, including death and others as set out in the company's Articles of Association.

In what capacity does a director act?

A director acts in two capacities:

1. as an agent, a capacity which imposes duties of loyalty and good faith on the director;

2. as a trustee of the company's money and property.

In the director an employee?

If the director has a contract of service he will also be an employee of the company.

It is preferable that all executive directors have a contract of service. If no written contract exists, a written memorandum setting out the terms should be kept. Such contracts may not exceed five years in duration unless agreed by the shareholders in general meeting. In general these contracts of service, or the written memoranda of terms, must be made available for inspection by the members.

Does age matter?

There is a provision in the Companies Act 1985 for directors of public companies, or of subsidiaries of public companies, who are over the age of 70 to be re-elected each year by the shareholders in general meeting. This provision may, however, be overriden by an appropriate clause in the Articles of Association of the company.

Who cannot be a director?

An undischarged bankrupt, unless approved by the court; anyone disqualified by a court order; and the company's auditor cannot become a director of a company.

What happens in a group?

The directors of a subsidiary company are responsible for the affairs of that company. However, where the subsidiary is effectively controlled and managed by its parent, the directors of the parent may be deemed to be shadow directors of the subsidiary.

Can an individual be a director of more than one company?

Nothing in the Companies Acts restricts the number of directorships an individual may have. However, directors' service contracts often impose restrictions, eg on directorships in the same group or non-conflicting companies. Furthermore, individuals should think carefully before accepting additional appointments to ensure that they can devote sufficient time to each directorship to carry out their duties and responsibilities properly.

2   Directors' powers

What powers do directors have?

Directors will be authorised to manage the business of the company. As such, they may take any decision necessary, provided that it is in accordance with the company's own 'rules' as stated in its Memorandum and Articles of Association, and with the Companies Acts. These documents should therefore be studied carefully by all directors to ensure that transactions entered into are valid.

Directors must exercise their powers on a collective basis, majority decisions prevailing. Directors acting without the authority of the board may be liable for breach of duty to the company. They may also be liable to any third party who, as a result of the directors' actions, has suffered a loss.

3 The board of directors

How does the board operate?

The board exercises a collective responsibility to ensure that the company's affairs are conducted properly. Individual directors must therefore cooperate with each other and respect the decisions of the board.

What is the significance of board meetings?

As a result of the Insolvency Act 1986 and the Company Directors Disqualification Act 1986, it is important for directors to be able to demonstrate that they have acted properly.

Accordingly, it is no longer adequate for important company decisions to be taken as a result of informal, undocumented discussions. Regular board meetings should be held with prearranged agendas. For valid decisions to be taken, a quorum (as defined by the Articles of Association of the company) should be present. All discussions and decisions should be properly documented, and the minutes circulated to the directors.

Directors need to be able to demonstrate that at all times they are aware of the company's trading position and financial status, and should document the consideration they give to the company's future prospects.

Can directors delegate their powers?

It would not be practical for all decisions which arise in the day-to-day running of the company to be taken at board meetings. It is therefore usual for the board to appoint one of its members as managing director, and to delegate to him the power to make such decisions.

4   Duties of a director

What duties do directors have?

The principal duty of a director is owed to the company on whose behalf the director acts as agent.

Directors have a fiduciary duty similar to that of a trustee. In return for the powers entrusted to them, directors must act honestly and show loyalty and good faith to the company. At all times conflicts of interest between themselves and the company must be avoided. If any such conflict arises, a director may be held to be personally liable to the company for any loss it has suffered, or the director may have to account for any benefit gained.

Directors are expected to display the skill and care that a reasonable person carrying out the same functions would display. The degree of skill expected of a director will be determined by the courts, having regard to the qualifications of the individual director. Thus, more will be expected of experienced business individuals and professionally qualified persons than of inexperienced persons.

In addition to the above, there are also various statutory duties imposed on directors by company law. These include such areas as preparation of the annual financial statements (discussed below) and consideration of the interests of employees. The latter are enforceable upon the directors by the company, not the individual employees, and are intended to ensure that employees are fairly treated in all respects.

What happens if there is a breach of duty?

Directors who fail to fulfil their duties have unlimited liability for any resultant loss suffered by the company. This is discussed later in the book in more detail.

What responsibility do directors have for financial statements and returns?

Directors are responsible for presenting the company's annual financial statements to the shareholders. The responsibility for preparing these financial statements rests solely with the directors, although assistance may be obtained (in practice this is frequently obtained from the company's auditors). Such assistance does not, however, result in a sharing of the responsibility for preparing the financial statements; this remains with the directors.

The annual financial statements must contain a considerable amount of detail regarding the directors. The aim of this statutory requirement is to ensure that the shareholders are fully aware of any benefits the directors may have obtained as a direct result of their office.

If the financial statements are approved by the directors and one or more of them knows that the financial statements do not comply with the Companies Acts, or any of the directors is reckless in their approach to the financial statements, that director could be liable to a fine. In order for directors to have a defence against prosecution they must show that they took all reasonable steps to prevent the financial statements from being approved. This dissent should be minuted.

The directors are also responsible for making annual returns to the Registrar of Companies. Additional returns may be required during the year, eg if there is a change in a directorship.

Directors should be aware that time restrictions exist for statutory requirements such as the filing of annual financial statements and making returns to the Registrar of Companies. Penalties by way of fines may be imposed for late filing of returns with the Registrar of Companies on the company and its directors, secretary, manager, or other persons in accordance with whose instructions the directors are accustomed to act.

In the case of late filing of financial statements with the Registrar of Companies the fines imposed on the company are automatic and vary depending on the time elapsed since the passing of the filing deadline (ie ten months from the accounting reference date for private companies, and seven months for public companies):

	Public Co.s	Private Co.s
Not more than 3 months	£500	£100
3–6 months	£1000	£250
6–12 months	£2000	£500
More than 12 months	£5000	£1000

Persistent breaches of the Companies Acts' requirements to file returns, financial statements, or other documents with the Registrar may result in disqualification from holding the office of a director for up to five years.

What accounting records must be kept?

Directors also have a statutory duty to keep proper and accessible books of account which show at any time an up-to-date picture of the company's financial position. In particular, the accounting records must contain:

- details of all monetary transactions;

- records of all the company's assets and liabilities;

- for companies dealing in goods, statements of stock at the year-end together with supporting stock-taking details;

- with the exception of goods sold in ordinary retail trade, statements of all goods purchased and sold, with adequate detail to allow identification of sellers and buyers.

Can directors trade with their company?

It is essential that directors do not abuse their position by gaining advantage from transactions with the company.

The Articles of Association of a company usually contain

certain provisions covering such transactions, and lay down the procedures to be followed.

In addition, complex rules are laid down by statute concerning a company entering various transactions, and these are discussed later in the book.

5 Insolvency

When is a company insolvent?

A company is deemed to be insolvent not only if it is unable to pay its debts as they fall due but also if the value of its assets is less than that of its liabilities including contingent and prospective liabilities.

What actions should directors take if they think their company is insolvent?

When a company is faced with insolvency the board of directors should seek specialist professional advice before deciding on the best course of action in order to minimise potential losses and their personal exposure. Any decisions taken should be documented. Alternatives would normally include:

- selling the business as a going concern;

- entering into a voluntary arrangement where the directors make a proposal to the creditors with regard to a scheme of arrangement, eg to reduce their claims. All creditors are entitled to vote on the proposed scheme. However, any changes in the rights of secured or preferential creditors cannot be approved without their separate agreement. A scheme proposed by the directors must first be considered by a person who is qualified to act as a liquidator under the Insolvency Act 1986;

- requesting the appointment of an administrative receiver ('receiver'), who is defined as a person appointed by a secured creditor under a floating charge. The exact scope of a receiver's powers will be determined by reference to the debenture under which the receiver is appointed. Under the Insolvency Act the receiver is given the power to run the business of the company and as such is the agent of the company. Obviously, the receiver's primary purpose is to recover the amounts owed to the secured creditor, and this may be achieved by the sale of the company's assets caught under the charge;

- requesting the appointment of an administrator who can take charge of the company's affairs on behalf of all its creditors as an alternative to liquidation. The administrator is appointed by the court and is given powers similar to those of a receiver to manage the company, and may also remove and appoint directors. The court must be satisfied that the company faced serious financial difficulties and that the administration is likely to achieve the survival of the company in whole or part, or that there will be a more advantageous realisation than would otherwise be achieved;

- winding up or liquidating the company. This effectively brings its corporate life to an end and may be either a compulsory winding up by the court or a voluntary winding up by either its members or creditors. The more common method is voluntary winding up, although both involve a liquidator realising assets, agreeing claims, investigating the affairs of the company and its directors (unless it is a members' voluntary liquidation), and distributing available funds to creditors. Any remaining surplus is then distributed to the shareholders.

Can directors restart their business under a similar name?

A person who has been a director of a company at any time in the 12 months leading up to an insolvent liquidation may not become a director or otherwise be involved with a company or business with a similar, or the same, name as the liquidated company within five years of the start of the liquidation, except with court approval or in accordance with the exceptions included in the Insolvency Rules 1986, eg acquisition of the same name from the liquidator.

The penalty for breach of these provisions is a fine or prison sentence or both.

What are the tax consequences of a company's going into liquidation?

The commencement of winding up terminates a corporation tax accounting period. It is important to realise this, as tax payments and various time limits for claims for relief are linked in time to the end of the accounting period.

Generally, on the appointment of a liquidator, the company ceases to have beneficial ownership of its assets. This means that, if the company is the parent of a group, the tax groupings for group relief and dividend/interest payments gross etc will be broken up. It is specifically provided that capital gains tax groupings are generally not broken on the commencement of a winding up.

A VAT return is required to be made up to the date of the appointment of a liquidator. After this, normal return periods are used for accounting for VAT.

Distributions by a liquidator are capital payments, and, as such, Advance Corporation Tax is not accountable.

An administration order and the appointment of a receiver do not have any direct tax consequences.

6 Disqualification of directors

When would a director be disqualified?

The Company Directors Disqualification Act 1986 gives the courts power to issue disqualification orders prohibiting an individual from acting as a director of a company or having any connection with the setting up or management of a company.

Disqualification will be ordered where the court finds that a director's or shadow director's conduct renders him unfit to be concerned in the management of a company, ie where fraudulent trading or persistent breaches of corporate legislation have occurred.

How long is the period of disqualification?

Disqualification can be for any period between 2 and 15 years.

When is disqualification considered?

The Secretary of State for Trade and Industry will ask the court to make a disqualification order where he considers it appropriate after reviewing reports made by the following:

- an administrator, receiver or, where the company has gone into insolvent liquidation, a liquidator;

- an inspector appointed under the Companies Act 1985 or the Financial Services Act 1986 to investigate the affairs of the company or individuals connected with it.

What factors are taken into account?

In deciding whether a director or shadow director should be disqualified, the court will take into account:

- any misfeasance or breach of any fiduciary or other duty by the director in relation to the company;

- any misapplication or retention by the director of, or any conduct by the director giving rise to an obligation to account for, any money or other property of the company;

- the extent of the director's responsibility for any failure to:

  - prepare annual financial statements and to sign the balance sheet;
  - keep proper accounting records;
  - keep the accounting records in the proper place and preserve them for the period specified in the Companies Acts;
  - maintain an up-to-date register of directors and secretaries;
  - keep the register of members in the proper place;
  - make an annual return at the proper time;
  - register charges created by the company;

- the extent of the director's responsibility for the company's becoming insolvent;

- the extent of the director's responsibility for any failure by the company to supply any goods or services which have been paid for in whole or in part;

- the extent of the director's responsibility for the company's entering into any transaction giving preference to a creditor or any other transaction which is liable to be set aside;

- the extent of the director's responsibility for any failure by the directors to call a creditors' meeting in a creditors' voluntary winding up;

- any failure by the director to comply with the requirements as to the statement of affairs to be prepared by the company and submitted to the receiver or liquidator;

- any failure by the director to cooperate with the liquidator.

What happens if a disqualified person becomes a director?

Any person who is disqualified from managing companies will become personally liable for any debts of any company which the individual manages, and on conviction by the courts may also be imprisoned for up to two years, or fined, or both.

7 Liabilities of a director

What is the extent of a director's liability?

Unlike shareholders, whose liability to the company is limited to any unpaid amount on the shares for which they have subscribed, a director's liability is unlimited. If a director is also a shareholder, his liability may therefore be twofold.

Any attempt by the company to exempt a director from any liability in respect of negligence or breach of duty is void under the Companies Acts.

In certain circumstances a director can be made personally liable to the company for acts of fraud or negligence, and there is no limit to the damages for which such a director may be liable to the company or to a third party.

When will a director be liable to third parties?

Directors are liable to pay compensation to anyone who has invested in their company as a result of false or misleading statements in a prospectus or equivalent documentation.

Directors may also be liable if they fail to make clear in their dealings with third parties that they are acting on behalf of their company, or if they make fraudulent misrepresentations.

Can directors insure against their liability?

Directors may now insure against their potential liabilities to the company, shareholders, and third parties in general. This is a relatively new advance for directors, and professional advice should be sought prior to taking out such an insurance policy.

A company is not prevented from purchasing and maintaining insurance for any officer in respect of his possible liability. However, this fact must be stated in the directors' report which accompanies the annual financial statements. Such a payment may be a benefit in kind for the directors concerned.

Can directors protect themselves by resigning?

Resignation on its own will not protect a director from personal liability. Where there is a disagreement, the dissenting director should ensure that his views are fully reflected in the minutes of the directors' meetings before resigning.

When can directors be asked to contribute to their company's assets?

Under the Insolvency Act 1986 a director may be asked to contribute to a company's assets where that company has gone into insolvent liquidation and at some time before the commencement of the winding up the director knew or ought to have concluded that there was no reasonable prospect of the company's avoiding liquidation.

Under the civil offence of wrongful trading, a director will not be liable if it can be shown that every reasonable step was taken that ought to have been taken to minimise any loss to creditors.

On what basis will they be judged?

A director's actions will be judged by comparison with:

- the expected actions and conclusions reached by a reasonably diligent person, having the knowledge, skill and experience that may be expected of a person carrying out the director's function;

- the knowledge, skill and experience that the director actually has.

The standard of care required of a director is highly subjective and is difficult to define with certainty. There is an implication that a higher standard of care is required from a professionally qualified director. Where it is apparent to a liquidator that an offence has been committed by a director, the court will determine the exact scope of the standard of care in the light of the individual circumstances of that case. Errors of judgement do not constitute negligent conduct and the courts will not judge past conduct in the light of knowledge which was not reasonably available at the time.

However, all directors should take a close interest in their company's financial state and document the consideration they give to the company's future prospects. These provisions apply equally to all directors, including non-executive directors (who may generally not be involved in the day-to-day affairs of the business) and shadow directors (whose instructions and directions are followed by the directors).

What is fraudulent trading?

The Companies Act 1985 includes the criminal offence of fraudulent trading. This offence is committed by a person who is knowingly a party to the carrying on of business with the intent to defraud creditors of the company. If convicted, such a person can be sentenced to imprisonment, or a fine, or both. It must be borne in mind that it is not necessary for the company to be the object of insolvency proceedings, and that the offence may be committed at any time by the director.

The Insolvency Act 1986 contains a civil offence, also for fraudulent trading, which imposes a personal liability to contribute to a company's assets on conviction. Proceedings may be commenced only by application to the court by a liquidator in the process of winding up a company.

What is the difference between fraudulent and wrongful trading?

Both the criminal and civil offences of fraudulent trading require a heavy burden of proof, with the necessity to prove a clear intention to defraud, ie dishonesty as distinct from recklessness or incompetence. The intention to defraud will occur if the company carries on business and incurs debts at a time when there is, to the knowledge of the directors, no reasonable prospect of the creditors ever receiving payment.

The civil offence of wrongful trading does not require a fraudulent intent to be established, and it is therefore likely to be applied more frequently than either the civil or criminal offence of fraudulent trading.

8 Directors' remuneration

On what basis are directors paid?

A company's Articles of Association usually allow for the payment of directors' remuneration. Alternatively, or in addition, a director's contract of service may specify the amount to be paid. If the amount is not specified, directors' remuneration is voted annually by the board of directors and must subsequently be approved by the members in general meeting.

Directors' remuneration is distinguished from directors' fees for services. There must be provision in a company's Articles of Association for such fees to be paid.

What is the tax position?

PAYE must be deducted from directors' remuneration at the time of payment. It is prohibited by the Companies Act 1985 for directors to receive gross remuneration. Directors are taxed at the point at which the money becomes available to them, ie on the earliest of the following dates:

- when payment is actually made;
- when the director is entitled to be paid;
- when the director's earnings are credited in the company records;
- if the amount of the director's earnings for a particular period is determined before the end of a period, at the end of that period;
- if the amount is determined after the period ends, when the earnings are determined.

The company will be allowed to charge a director's remuneration against profits for corporation tax purposes only where that remuneration has been paid to the director within nine months of the accounting period's end. If the remuneration is paid after this date, the expense is deductible in the year it is paid.

In some situations a director's remuneration may be paid to a partnership or company controlled by the director.

Although director's fees received by a partnership where directorships are held by partners are strictly assessable under Schedule E, in practice they may be included in the Schedule D assessment, provided:

- the directorships are held as a normal part of the profession;

- the fees are a small part of the profits;

- the fees are shared among the partners.

Furthermore, fees received by a company in respect of a director's services to other companies may generally, by agreement with the Inland Revenue, be treated as part of its income and not be subject to PAYE.

Tax is not charged in respect of awards made to directors as testimonials to mark long service which take the form of tangible articles or of shares in any employing company of reasonable cost, when the relevant period of service is not less than 20 years and no similar award has been made to the recipient within the previous 10 years.

In addition to remuneration, benefits in kind and expenses must be reported to the Inland Revenue by the company, usually on Form P11D. Such items include all reimbursements of expenses by the company to the director, as well as expenses incurred by the director but paid for by the company. It is then up to each director to agree with the Inland Revenue how much of these items constitute personal benefit and how much is pure business expense incurred in the course of his duties as a director. In practice, no assessment is made in respect of removal expenses borne by the employer where the employee has to change his residence in order to take up new employ-ment, or as a result of a transfer to another post within an employer's organisation, provided that the expenses are reasonable in amount and their payment is properly controlled.

The cost of travelling from home to work is generally not tax-deductible. By concession, this rule is modified in the following circumstances:

Table 1 Tax allowance on travel expenditure

Nature of expenses	Tax position
Travel between their base and other group or associated companies	Expense is tax allowable
Travelling expenses paid to directors who provide their services without remuneration to a company not managed with a view to dividends	The cost is not treated as assessable
Expenses incurred by directors carrying out their duties where directorships are held as a part of a professional practice	Allowed as deductions in assessing the profits of the practice

Provided certain complex rules are complied with, termination payments up to a limited amount can be paid tax-free. Termination payments are usually exempt from National Insurance payments.

9 Transactions with directors

What are the rules governing transactions between a company and its directors?

The legislation is summarised as follows:

- Companies are prohibited from making loans to directors or guaranteeing their loans.

- For relevant companies, the provisions prohibiting loans and guarantees are extended to cover those made to connected persons.

- Indirect arrangements, for example, a loan to a third party which makes a loan to the director, are also prohibited, thus preventing the rules from being avoided by such arrangements.

- In general, all transactions with directors, whether legal or illegal, must be disclosed in the financial statements.

The intention of the legislation which prohibits the above transactions is to protect the interests of shareholders and other third parties. Thus, certain transactions will remain illegal, whether or not the shareholders approve them, in order to protect the interests of creditors and minority shareholders.

The legislation relates to all companies registered under the Companies Acts. Companies registered overseas are exempt, even if they have a place of business in the UK. However, a parent company which is registered under the Companies Acts and which has a subsidiary registered overseas must comply with the legislation and disclosure requirements for transactions between the subsidiary and the directors of the parent company.

A company's Memorandum and Articles of Association may be more restrictive than the legislation and should therefore be consulted before any transactions are entered into with directors.

What is a relevant company?

A 'relevant company' is defined as being any company which is either:

- a public company; or
- a member of a group which contains a public company.

What is a connected person?

The term 'connected persons' broadly includes the following:

- a director's spouse, children, and stepchildren under the age of 18, except where they are themselves directors of the company;
- companies in which the director and persons connected with that director collectively control 20 per cent of the nominal share capital or 20 per cent of the voting power of the company;
- partners of the director;
- trustees of any settlement in which the director or persons connected with that director are beneficiaries.

The definition of connected persons does not extend to the parents, brothers, or sisters of the director. Nor does it include trustees of a settlement by the director if neither the director nor persons connected with the director are beneficiaries.

Can a company make a loan to a director?

In general, a company should not make loans or provide guarantees or security in connection with loans made by third parties to directors (including shadow directors), or enter into any direct or indirect arrangements regarding such transactions for its directors or those of its parent company. For relevant companies, the legislation is extended to prohibit similar transactions with connected persons.

What is a loan?

Legislation does not provide a definition of a loan. The definition put forward by the courts, and used until legislation states otherwise, is taken from *The Shorter Oxford English Dictionary*, which states:

> A loan is a sum of money lent for a time to be returned in money or money's worth.

Thus, for a transaction to be treated as a loan, there must be an intention that the amount will be repaid.

Is it only loans that are restricted?

Quasi-loans and credit transactions are also prohibited for relevant companies, together with any associated guarantees or arrangements.

Quasi-loans are payments or undertakings to pay amounts on behalf of a director by the company, the director subsequently reimbursing the company. A typical example of this type of loan is the use of company credit cards for personal expenditure by a director.

Credit transactions are those where payment in full does not occur at the time of sale or at the date on which the transaction was entered into. These will arise when the company:

- supplies goods or sells land under a hire-purchase agreement or contract sale;

- leases or hires any land or goods in return for periodic payments;

- disposes of land or supplies goods or services on deferred-payment terms.

Are there any exclusions?

The following transactions are excluded from the above rules:

- transactions between a company and the directors of its subsidiary, or transactions between a company and the directors of fellow subsidiaries, if the directors are not also directors of the parent company. For relevant companies this will also include connected persons;

- loans to directors where the aggregate of the relevant amount is less than £5000. Guarantees and similar arrangements are not included in the relevant amount. For relevant companies this exclusion is not extended to loans to connected persons;

- quasi-loans made to directors of relevant companies if the total amount outstanding at any time is less than £5000 and the director is required to repay each quasi-loan within two months of its inception. Quasi-loans entered into by relevant companies with persons connected with directors are not included in this exemption;

- credit transactions with directors and connected persons of relevant companies if the aggregate relevant amount does not exceed £10,000. In addition, all credit transactions of any value will be permitted if they are in the ordinary course of business and the value and terms of the transactions are in accordance with normal trading;

- loans, quasi-loans, and credit transactions, or guarantees or security for any such transactions entered into by a company with its holding company. Loans and quasi-loans may be made to any company in the same group even though that other company may be a connected person of a director;

- loans, guarantees, and arrangements provided to meet expenditure by the director for the purpose of company business or for the purpose of enabling the director to perform his duties as an officer of the company properly. This exemption also extends to quasi-loans and credit

Table 2 Permitted transactions for directors and connected persons

	Public company or member of group containing public company	Private company not member of group containing public company
Loans	Up to £5000 per director and up to £20,000 to meet business expenses (prior approval of shareholders or must be repaid within six months). May not be made to connected persons.	Up to £5000 per director. May be made to a connected person. Unlimited funds to meet business expenses (prior approval of shareholders or must be repaid within six months).
Quasi-loans	If reimbursable within two months and total per director less than £5000. May not be made to connected persons.	No restriction
Credit Transactions	If under normal commercial terms or total outstanding per director less than £10,000.	No restriction

Note: different rules apply to moneylending companies

transactions for relevant company directors. For relevant companies only, the aggregate relevant amount of any such transaction should not exceed £20,000.

The exemption will apply (for all companies) only if the transaction is approved by the shareholders in general meeting, although funds may be provided on the basis that if the transaction is not subsequently approved all amounts will be repaid within six months.

Additional exemptions exist for money-lending companies and recognised banks. These exemptions are not considered further in this book.

What is the relevant amount?

The relevant amount of a transaction or arrangement is the total of all existing transactions or arrangements of a particular type entered into with a director and that individual's connected persons.

The relevant amount aggregates the following:

- the value of the proposed transaction or arrangement;

- the value of any existing permitted indirect arrangement of the same type;

- the value of any previous permitted transaction of the same type less any amount paid.

In aggregating amounts, illegal transactions should not be included.

When is shareholder approval required?

In addition to the above, prior approval by the shareholders is generally required for any substantial property transactions between any company and a director of the company, or its parent company, or a person connected with such a director.

The provisions relate to transactions involving substantial non-cash assets, the value of which is both greater than £2000 and exceeds the lower of 10 per cent of the company's assets or £100,000.

No prior approval will be required where the company concerned in the transaction is a wholly owned subsidiary and the director is not a director of the parent company. Transfers of assets between subsidiaries and parent companies can also be made without prior approval.

There are additional rules affecting such transactions by companies which are subject to regulation by the International Stock Exchange.

What are the liabilities for breach of the rules?

A breach of the rules by a company and/or a director will result in a liability being owed either to a third party, or to the company, or both. In addition, damaging publicity to the company could follow from civil or criminal actions.

A director or connected person will be deemed to have committed an offence if that individual authorises or allows a company to enter into a transaction or arrangement knowing, or having reasonable cause to know, that the company was breaching the legislation.

Civil remedies may include the company or third party's being able to rescind the transaction and recover the asset or money involved.

This can be done only if:

- it is possible to replace the asset or money;

- the rights of any third parties, who entered into the transaction in good faith and gave consideration, would not be affected; and

- the company has not been indemnified by the director for any loss or damage suffered;

Criminal actions may follow if relevant companies and their directors enter into prohibited transactions or arrangements. Conviction on indictment can result in a maximum prison sentence of two years or a fine. Summary convictions may lead to a maximum prison sentence of six months or a maximum fine of £2000.

What are the tax effects of a loan?

Generally a loan to a director may give rise to a benefit in kind reportable on a form P11D and assessable on the director. The benefit is quantified by imputing interest at a prescribed rate to the loan and deducting any loan interest paid and making an allowance for interest payments which if made would be tax-deductible. There is also a *de-minimis* exemption.

Where the loan to the director is from a close company and the director is a participator in that company, then an amount equivalent to Advance Corporation Tax (ACT) on a dividend equal to the loan generally must be made to the Inland Revenue. When the loan or part thereof is repaid, the ACT equivalent or part thereof is repayable by the Inland Revenue. Interest and penalties may be chargeable on late payments of the ACT equivalent.

What about share transactions?

A director is not prohibited by law from holding shares and debentures in the company of which he is a director, although the Articles of Association of the company may contain such a prohibition.

However, directors are prohibited from buying options to purchase or sell their company's shares or debentures if they are listed on a stock exchange, although they may purchase a right to subscribe for shares, for example, under an approved scheme. There are no rules in the Companies Acts relating to the holding of such interests other than the disclosure requirements, which are considered later. Directors of companies which are subject to the rules of the International Stock Exchange must also comply with the 'Model Code for Securities Transactions by Directors of Listed Companies'. The 'Model Code' restricts the periods in which directors can trade in their company's shares and states that directors should not deal in the shares on considerations of a short-term nature.

For an Inland Revenue approved executive share option scheme, there is no tax charge on the individual on acquisition of the option or the shares, provided options are exercised in accordance with the scheme. On disposal, there will be a capital gains tax charge based on the difference between the proceeds and acquisition cost plus indexation.

For unapproved share option schemes, where the option is not capable of being exercised more than seven years after it is obtained, there is no tax charge on the grant of the option. There is an income tax charge on the exercise of the option based on the difference between the market value of the shares and the value paid. Additionally, income tax charges can arise in respect of increases in value of the shares after acquisition. If the option is capable of being exercised later than seven years after it is obtained, a tax charge can arise on the grant of the option.

Great care should be taken by directors who hold company shares and debentures to ensure that they do not become involved in insider dealing.

Insider dealing is the use of insider information by any individual, director or otherwise, in order to make a profit or avoid a loss on transactions in marketable securities. This will apply primarily to companies whose shares or debentures are quoted on a recognised stock exchange.

'Insider information' is the term used to describe unpublished, confidential information which, if published, could affect the price of the company's shares or debentures.

Directors form an important group of individuals who are most likely to have insider information available to them. Directors taking advantage of such information, acquired as a result of their position, will be in breach of their duties to the company.

Insider dealing is a criminal offence, and directors have a responsibility to ensure that they, the company's employees, and the company's agents comply with the statutory legislation.

10 Disclosure of transactions

What are the disclosure requirements?

It is important that shareholders be fully aware of any potential conflicts which may arise between a director's responsibilities to the company and his own personal interests. To this end, a considerable amount of disclosure is required in a company's financial statements. If the disclosure requirements are not met, it is the duty of the auditors to highlight this in their audit report to the shareholders.

Subject to certain defined exceptions, the financial statements must disclose any transactions, whether legal or not, which occurred at any time during the year between a director (or a person connected with the director) and the company. This includes transactions entered into during the year even though there are no amounts outstanding at the year-end or loans made in a previous period which are outstanding at the beginning of the year. The legality of a transaction is determined at the time it takes place — for example, a loan made to an employee who subsequently becomes a director must be disclosed but is not illegal.

It should be noted that there are no differences in the disclosure requirements for private or public companies.

Does it make a difference if the transaction is illegal?

As stated above, the disclosures relate to transactions whether legal or not. Furthermore, there is no statutory requirement to indicate in the financial statements whether or not a transaction is illegal. However, disclosure may be required in order for the financial statements to show a true and fair view, and any particular situation should be discussed with the company's auditors.

What amount must be disclosed?

Where transactions entered into during the year exceed the exempt amounts outlined below, all the transactions of that type must be disclosed, not just the excess over the exempt amount.

What happens in a group?

A company's financial statements must disclose transactions between the following parties:

- the company and its directors and their connected persons;
- the company's subsidiaries and its directors and connected persons;
- the company, its subsidiaries, and the directors and their connected persons, of any parent company of the company.

Details of transactions entered into between a company or its subsidiaries and the directors of the subsidiary need not be disclosed, provided that the director is not also a director of the company or its parent company.

In a group of companies, these requirements may result in the duplication of disclosure, as illustrated by the following example:

Assume the following vertical group structure with each company having one director:

Company	Directors
A	X
↓	
B	Y
↓	
C	Z

- Company A will disclose transactions between director X and companies A, B, and C.

- Company B will disclose transactions between directors X and Y and companies B and C.

- Company C will disclose transactions between directors X, Y, and Z and company C.

What are the specific disclosure requirements for transactions with directors?

For all transactions requiring disclosure, the following details must be given:

- the fact that the transaction took place;

- the name of the director concerned, and if the transaction was with a connected person of a director, the name of that person;

- the principal terms of the transaction, for example, interest rates;

- any additional disclosures required as detailed below.

Individual transactions must be disclosed separately for each of the directors who held office for any period of time during the financial year.

The financial statements must disclose, where appropriate:

- loans, quasi-loans, credit transactions, and indirect arrangements;

- agreements to enter into such contracts;

- guarantees or security for loans;

- other transactions or arrangements in which a director has a material interest, whether that interest is direct or indirect.

What are the additional disclosure requirements for loans?

The following additional details must be disclosed for loans, agreements for loans, and indirect loans:

- the amount outstanding at the beginning and end of the financial year;

- the maximum balance outstanding during the financial year;

- any interest due on the loan but unpaid at the year-end;

- any provision included in the financial statements for potential non-recovery of either capital or interest, or both.

What are the additional disclosure requirements for guarantees or security for loans?

Additional details to be disclosed for guarantees or security for loans, whether direct or indirect, are the following:

- the liability of the company or subsidiary at the beginning and the end of the financial year;

- the maximum amount for which the company or subsidiary may become liable;

- any amounts paid or liabilities incurred by the company or subsidiary during the financial year in fulfilling the guarantee or in discharging the security given.

What are the additional disclosure requirements for quasi-loans and credit transactions?

For quasi-loans, credit transactions and related arrangements and agreements not exempt from the disclosure the following additional details must be given:

- the value of the transaction or arrangement; or

- the value of the transaction to which the agreement relates.

There is no requirement to disclose the amount outstanding at the beginning or end of the financial year.

Credit transactions, or any guarantees, security, or arrangements for such transactions, made by a company (or by a

Table 3 Summary of disclosure requirements for transactions with directors

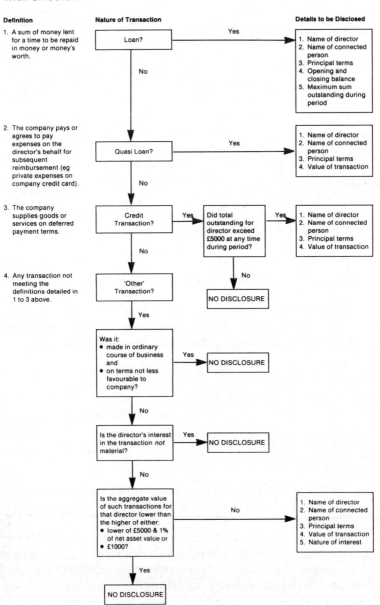

Definition

1. A sum of money lent for a time to be repaid in money or money's worth.

2. The company pays or agrees to pay expenses on the director's behalf for subsequent reimbursement (eg private expenses on company credit card).

3. The company supplies goods or services on deferred payment terms.

4. Any transaction not meeting the definitions detailed in 1 to 3 above.

Nature of Transaction

Loan? — Yes / No

Quasi Loan? — Yes / No

Credit Transaction? — Yes / No

Yes — Did total outstanding for director exceed £5000 at any time during period? — Yes / No

No — NO DISCLOSURE

'Other' Transaction? — Yes

Was it:
- made in ordinary course of business and
- on terms not less favourable to company?

Yes — NO DISCLOSURE

No

Is the director's interest in the transaction *not* material? — Yes — NO DISCLOSURE

No

Is the aggregate value of such transactions for that director lower than the higher of either:
- lower of £5000 & 1% of net asset value or
- £1000?

No

Yes — NO DISCLOSURE

Details to be Disclosed

1. Name of director
2. Name of connected person
3. Principal terms
4. Opening and closing balance
5. Maximum sum outstanding during period

1. Name of director
2. Name of connected person
3. Principal terms
4. Value of transaction

1. Name of director
2. Name of connected person
3. Principal terms
4. Value of transaction

1. Name of director
2. Name of connected person
3. Principal terms
4. Value of transaction
5. Nature of interest

subsidiary of the company) in relation to a director of that company or its parent company (or connected persons) need not be disclosed if the aggregate amount outstanding at any time during the year was less than £5000.

What are the additional disclosure requirements for material interests in other transactions?

A director is required by law to notify fellow directors as soon as possible of any interest he has in contracts entered into by the company.

For a transaction which does not fall into one of the categories above (ie an 'other' transaction), no disclosure is required where the interest is deemed not to be material by the other directors. The decision must take into account the relevance of the interest to the users of the financial statements and the value of the director's interest.

There is also an exemption from disclosure for other transactions into which the company enters in the ordinary course of business and on terms no less favourable to the company than if the directors had not been interested.

Additionally, material interests in other transactions are exempt from disclosure where the aggregate amount is:

- lower than £1000; or

- greater than £1000 but does not exceed the greater of £5000 or 1 per cent of the company's net assets.

Disclosure is required regardless of whether or not the transaction has been approved by the shareholders in general meeting.

No disclosure is required of other transactions in which the director's interest arose solely as a result of his being a director of both companies involved.

Contracts of service between a director and a company or its parent company or any subsidiary do not require disclosure in the financial statements (except for companies which are listed on the International Stock Exchange).

The further details required to be disclosed for 'other' transactions which are not exempt are as follows:

- the value of the transaction;
- the nature of the director's interest.

What are the disclosure requirements for share and debenture transactions?

The directors' report attached to the financial statements must include details of directors' interests in the shares and debentures (including options) of the company and other group companies. The disclosure is required in respect of people who were directors at the year-end and must include their interest at the year-end and the beginning of the year or, if appointed during the year, at the date of appointment. The International Stock Exchange additionally requires disclosure of any changes in the directors' interests after the year-end and an analysis of beneficial and non-beneficial interests.

The interests which must be disclosed are those which the Companies Acts require directors to disclose to the company and the company to record in the register of directors' interests. Directors are deemed to be interested in the shares owned by their spouses and children (including stepchildren) aged under 18. In addition they are also deemed to be interested in shares owned by a company of which they control one-third of the voting power as well as those owned by a trust of which they are a beneficiary. There are certain exemptions from disclosure, including shares held as a bare or custodian trustee.

What are the disclosure requirements for remuneration?

The financial statements must include the total amounts of directors' emoluments, directors' and past directors' pensions, and compensation paid for loss of office. The amounts should include all sums paid or payable by the company, any subsidiary, and any other person.

Directors' emoluments include any amount paid to or receivable by a person in respect of his services as a director of the company and in respect of services, while director of the company, as a director of a subsidiary. Emoluments include fees and percentages, any sum paid by way of expense allowance (in so far as these sums are chargeable to UK income tax), any contributions paid in respect of a director under a pension scheme, the estimated money value of any other benefits received by them otherwise than in cash, and any amounts paid to a person in respect of accepting the office of director (ie golden hellos).

Where the total amount required to be disclosed as emoluments is greater than £60,000 or the company is a member of a group, the remuneration of the chairman and the highest paid director, if different, must be disclosed. Remuneration is the total emoluments less the contributions to a pension scheme paid by the company. In addition, the number of directors receiving remuneration in each band of £5000, starting from £0 to £5000, must be disclosed, eg:

	1992	1991
£0–£5000	2	1
£5001–£10,000	–	1
£10,001–£15,000	2	1

Emoluments disclosed within the financial statements include amounts paid or payable to a person connected with, or a body corporate controlled by, the director.

Additionally, companies are required to disclose separately any consideration paid to or received by third parties for making available the services of any person as a director of the company or its subsidiary undertakings. Consideration includes the money value of benefits other than in cash. For this purpose, 'third parties' are persons other than:

- the director or a person connected with, or company controlled by, that director;

- the company or any of its subsidiary undertakings.

The amount disclosed in respect of compensation for loss of office must include the estimated money value of benefits other than in cash, and the nature of any benefit must be stated (eg a company director's being allowed to retain his company car).

The amount disclosed in respect of pensions to directors past and present must include the estimated money value of pension benefits which are other than in cash, and the nature of any benefits must be stated.

11 Practical implications for transactions with directors

What are the practical implications?

Consideration is given below to a number of areas relating to transactions with directors which should be considered in the light of the rules. This is not intended to be an exhaustive coverage, but indicates how the theoretical concepts may operate in practice. It is recommended that professional advice be sought when considering a particular situation.

There are no exceptions (other than for banks) which permit the provision of finance to directors of a company simply because it is on the same terms as similar arrangements made available to other employees. The provision of finance to directors must be in accordance with the rules previously discussed.

It should be noted that the exemptions for loans to finance the acquisition of a property apply to money-lending companies only.

What is the position on advances for business expenditure?

Care should be taken to ensure that advances against expenses are not greatly in excess of expenditure and that they do not remain outstanding over a long period of time.

An excessive advance for a long period might constitute a loan and hence require disclosure. In addition, if there are repeated advances (or one large advance) which are construed as loans, they are illegal if they exceed the specified limits.

What about directors' current accounts with the company?

Overdrawn directors' current accounts should not be offset at the year-end against any loans made by the director to the company unless evidence is available to indicate an intention by both parties that the loan should be settled in this manner.

Debit balances on directors' current accounts should be avoided as they may represent a loan which must be disclosed or indicate that there have been credit transactions or quasi-loans also requiring disclosure. In addition they may be treated as the equivalent of a distribution for tax purposes, and a benefit in kind may arise based on interest not charged.

Is remuneration drawn on account a loan?

Remuneration drawn on account again may constitute a loan to a director and therefore it is preferable that such a situation be avoided. It is essential, however, that if remuneration is drawn on account, PAYE and National Insurance contributions are deducted to comply with the regulations.

What about quasi-loans?

A typical example of a quasi-loan occurs when a company purchases a season ticket for a director and is reimbursed by monthly deductions from the director's salary. A method of avoiding such a purchase being deemed a quasi-loan is to provide the director with the cost of the season ticket and then seek reimbursement by the same means. This will constitute a loan for which there is no time limit on the repayments, in contrast to the two-month repayment period allowed for quasi-loans.

This type of structuring of transactions can be more attractive than a quasi-loan, although this is only of significance if the company is a public company or part of a group containing a public company.

Another example of a quasi-loan is the provision of company credit cards to directors for business and personal use, they reimburse the company for the personal element. Methods of avoiding the creation of such a quasi-loan include:

- the director's giving the company a cheque in settlement of any personal expenditure when the credit card statement is received;

- using two credit cards, one business and one personal, the director then being responsible for his personal expenditure.

12   Other legislation

What other legislation affects directors?

In addition to the rules imposed by company law, directors should also be aware of the large volume of additional legislation which exists.

A selection of the more important legislation and its impact on directors is considered below.

Taxation requirements

There are various taxes which a company may be liable to pay:

- Corporation tax will be due on any taxable profits made by the company. If the tax is not paid by the company, generally on the due date, an interest charge will arise. Penalties may also be imposed for failure to comply with obligations under corporation tax legislation, including failure to notify the inspector that the company is chargeable to corporation tax.

- PAYE and National Insurance contributions are collected from the employees by the company on behalf of the Inland Revenue. There may be penalties for late payment of monies due for which the company is liable. Interest may be charged on tax unpaid from 14 days after the end of the year of assessment to which the tax relates. Penalties may also be imposed for late filing of PAYE-related forms P35 and P11D. A P35 should generally be filed by 19 May and P11Ds by 6 June following the year of assessment.

- Companies satisfying certain criteria are required to make returns for VAT and, if appropriate, to pay the amounts required to HM Customs and Excise. In order to achieve this, companies are required by law to keep certain additional records to record VAT. Failure to do so will leave the company open to prosecution and financial penalties.

The company must generally also provide HM Customs and Excise with all the information it requests, producing documents if necessary, to avoid being prosecuted and subsequently fined.

Where it appears to the Commissioners of Customs and Excise that a company is liable to pay a civil penalty for VAT evasion where conduct involves dishonesty and that the conduct giving rise to the penalty is in whole or in part attributable to the dishonesty of a person who at the time was a director or managing officer of the company, the Commissioners may serve a notice on the named officer to recover the penalty. The company will then be assessable only in respect of any amount not assessed on the named officer.

Fraudulent evasion of all taxes is a criminal offence, as, generally, is providing false documents and information. Fines or terms of imprisonment may be imposed upon an individual responsible for such actions.

Health and Safety at Work Act 1974

This Act provides that where companies are held liable for breaches of the legislation, their officers, in certain circumstances, should also be liable.

Under the Act, duties are owed to both employees and other persons, and any breach of the law is a criminal offence.

A company and its directors are responsible for ensuring the health, safety, and welfare of all their employees. In addition the law requires that places also used by persons not employed by the company, eg car parks, must be safe.

Codes of practice are issued periodically to assist companies in establishing sound systems of health and safety measures. Although non-compliance with these codes alone is not a criminal offence, breaches may be cited against a company in a criminal action.

Data Protection Act 1984

The purpose of this Act is twofold:

1. to prevent the abuse of personal data;

2. to bring the UK legislation surrounding the electronic processing of personal data in line with that of other European countries.

The Act relates to any individual or organisation who or which processes electronically non-exempt personal data, and requires all such persons to register with the Data Protection Registrar.

It is the responsibility of all persons to ensure that the data they are using have been registered, unless such data are exempt, for the appropriate use and to implement suitable control measures to ensure data are maintained accurately. Thus, it is not solely the responsibility of the directors to register data uses, although, as persons entrusted with carrying on the business of the company, it is usual that they at least instigate registration.

It is a criminal offence for a person or organisation not to register. Non-registration may result in fines and the destruction of unregistered data.

Consumer Credit Act 1974

The purpose of the Consumer Credit Act is to regulate credit transactions by requiring providers of credit to be licensed and by imposing restrictions on the wording of advertisements.

Where a company provides credit, both it and the directors may be liable to criminal proceedings if they fail to register or otherwise comply with the Act.

Road Traffic Act 1972

Directors can be criminally liable if they do not make sure that all the company's vehicles are roadworthy and properly taxed and insured.

It is therefore essential that a system be established to ensure that all requirements of the Act are followed.

Environmental Protection Act 1990

Under environment protection legislation, directors and other officers can be personally liable for breaches of the Act.

The company must ensure that it is not violating pollution laws.

City Code on Takeovers and Mergers

Although not having the force of law, breaches of the 'City Code on Takeovers and Mergers' can lead to sanctions by the financial markets against companies and their directors and investigation by inspectors appointed by the Department of Trade and Industry.

The code broadly applies to quoted companies (ie companies which are listed by the Stock Exchange or have a quote on the Unlisted Securities Market operated by the International Stock Exchange) and governs the manner in which they may acquire shares in another company.

Conclusion

Directors, or potential directors, should consider carefully their role within the company and the duties and responsibilities attached.

Company directors are subject to extensive legislation relating to their duties to, and transactions with, the company. The overriding aim of the legislation is to protect the interests of shareholders and creditors by ensuring that directors do not abuse the powers entrusted to them. It should be noted that the rules must be followed even when the directors and the shareholders are the same group of people.

The legislation is complex and far-reaching, and all directors need to be aware of the requirements.

The protection afforded to creditors under the Insolvency Act and the extensive powers granted to the courts under the Company Directors Disqualification Act means that directors must consider their responsibilities very carefully. Ignorance of the statutory requirements will not be accepted as a valid excuse for non-compliance.

Civil and criminal liabilities may result from many varied circumstances, as highlighted in this book. Directors should therefore be aware of the detailed legislation and position as determined by the courts.

This book is written as a general guide and should not be relied upon for advice in specific cases. As any course of action will depend on individual circumstances, readers are strongly recommended to obtain professional advice to ensure that additional liabilities do not arise as a result of lack of knowledge or understanding.

Glossary

administrative receiver

An administrative receiver is a person appointed by a secured creditor under a floating charge to run the business of the company in order to recover amounts owed to the secured creditor. The receiver's powers will be determined by reference to the debenture under which the receiver is appointed.

administrator

An administrator is appointed by the court and is given powers similar to those of a receiver to manage the company on behalf of all creditors as an alternative to liquidation.

Advanced Corporation Tax (ACT)

When a company pays a dividend to its shareholders it must withhold advanced corporation tax (ACT) and pay it over to the Inland Revenue, so that the dividend is received net of tax by the shareholder.

ACT on dividends paid in a particular period may be set against a company's corporation tax liability of that period in certain circumstances.

agent

An agent is a person employed to act on behalf of another who is bound by such actions.

alternate director

An alternate director is appointed by a director and is empowered to perform the duties of that director, usually at board meetings, in the temporary absence of the appointing director.

annual accounts   Every company registered under the Companies Acts must prepare annual accounts (ie a balance sheet and profit and loss account) for each financial year which give a true and fair view. The annual accounts must be approved by the board of directors and laid before the members at the company's annual general meeting. A copy of the annual accounts must be filed with the Registrar of Companies for public inspection.

Annual General Meeting (AGM)   Every company must hold an annual general meeting of its shareholders in each calendar year and meetings may not be more than fifteen months apart. The purpose of the meeting will depend entirely on the articles of association of the company but usually the following matters will be dealt with:

- the declaration of a dividend;
- consideration of the financial statements;
- election of retiring directors;
- appointment of auditors and fixing their remuneration.

annual return   Every company must deliver to the Registrar of Companies an annual return each year which discloses general information about the company, its directors and shareholders.

Articles of Association   The Articles of Association is the constitutional document of a company setting out the internal regulations for the management of the company.

benefits in kind Benefits in kind are remuneration other than in the form of cash (eg company cars, loans, accommodation). They are relevant to disclosure of directors' emoluments and to directors' tax positions.

board of directors The power to run and manage a company is vested in its board of directors which is made up of all the directors.

charges over assets A company may offer certain of its creditors charges over its assets as security for its debts so that if the company defaults on its liability the secured creditor may appropriate the company's assets.

A fixed charge is attached to a specific item of the company's property which prevents the company from selling that item.

A floating charge is created in respect of circulating assets (eg cash, stock) to which it will not attach until crystallisation, ie some event causes it to be fixed. Before crystallisation unsecured debts can be paid out of the assets charged. After crystallization the charge is treated as fixed and therefore unsecured debts rank after those secured by the charge.

close company A close company is generally any UK resident company which is under the control of:

- five or fewer participants; or
- its participating directors.

Participants includes shareholders and their associates (eg ancestors, descendants, other immediate relatives, partners and certain trustees).

The original significance of close company status was to prevent companies being used to accumulate profits within the company rather than to distribute them to the individual shareholders, thus being subject to advantageous tax rates. Regulations sought to apportion profits to individual participators whether they were distributed or not.

However, the significance of close company status has been reduced with the abolition of the power to apportion profits for accounting periods beginning on or after 1 April 1989. However, close company status remains relevant in respect of:

- close investment holding companies;
- loans to participators;
- interest on loans to buy shares or lend to such companies being available for income tax relief;
- other minor tax consequences.

company

An association of persons formed for the purpose of some business or undertaking registered under the Companies Acts, having a separate legal personality recognised in law distinct from its membership, and therefore continues unaffected by changes in its membership.

company secretary

The company secretary is an officer of the company but is not, by virtue of the office, a member of the board of directors. The duties of the company secretary will vary according to the size of company, but will always include arranging and convening meetings and maintaining statutory registers. A company secretary may also be appointed a director of the company, but a sole director may not also be the secretary.

connected persons This term broadly includes the following:

- a director's spouse, children and step-children under the age of 18, except where they are themselves directors of the company;
- companies in which the director and persons connected with the director collectively control 20 per cent of the nominal share capital or 20 per cent of the voting power of the company;
- partners of the director;
- trustees of any settlement in which the director or persons connected with the director are beneficiaries.

The definition of connected persons does not extend to the parents, brothers or sisters of the director. Nor does it include trustees of a settlement by the director if neither the director nor persons connected with the director are beneficiaries.

contingent liability A contingency is a condition which exists at the balance sheet date, where the outcome will be confirmed only on the occurrence or non-occurrence of one or more uncertain future events. Examples of contingent liabilities include:

- guarantees given to third parties;
- legal actions pending;
- bills discounted with recourse.

credit transactions Credit transactions are those where payment in full does not occur at the time of sale or at the date on which the transaction was entered into. These will arise when the company:

- supplies goods or sells land under a hire purchase agreement or contract sale;
- leases or hires any land or goods in return for periodic payments;
- disposes of land or supplies goods or services on deferred payment terms.

debentures A debenture is a common form of borrowing by a company. They are bonds given under seal of the company, and evidence the fact that the company is liable to pay a specified amount with interest, and are generally charged upon the property of the company.

director A director is an officer of the company who, collectively with the other directors, is concerned with the management of the company.

directors' report Every company is required to prepare a directors' report for each financial year, to be delivered to the Registrar of Companies with the company's financial statements.

disqualification The Company Directors' Disqualification Act 1986 gives the courts power to issue disqualification orders prohibiting an individual from acting as a director of a company or having any connection with the setting up, or management, of a company.

Disqualification will be ordered where the court finds that a director's or shadow director's conduct renders them unfit to be concerned in the management of a company ie where fraudulent trading or persistent breaches of corporate legislation have occurred.

emoluments

Directors' emoluments include any amount paid to or receivable by a person in respect of their services as a director of the company and in respect of services, while director of the company, as a director of a subsidiary. Emoluments include fees and percentages, any sum paid by way of expense allowance (in so far as these sums are chargeable to UK income tax), any contributions paid in respect of a director under a pension scheme, the estimated money value of any other benefits received by the director otherwise than in cash, and any amounts paid to a person in respect of accepting the office of director (ie golden hellos).

executive director

An executive director is a person who, in addition to their position on the board, has managerial responsibilities for the day to day operations of the company.

extraordinary resolution

The Companies Act 1985 requires 75 per cent of those shareholders voting to vote in favour of an extraordinary resolution.

The company's articles may require an extraordinary resolution for any purpose other than one for which the Companies Act requires a special resolution.

Extraordinary resolutions are required by the Companies Acts in connection with certain aspects of winding up eg voluntary winding up.

fiduciary duty

Directors have a fiduciary duty, similar to that of a trustee. In return for the powers entrusted to them, the directors must act honestly and show loyalty and good faith to the company. At all time conflicts of interest between themselves and the company must be avoided. If any such conflict arises, a director may be held to be personally liable to the company for any loss it has suffered or the director may have to account for any benefit gained.

fraudulent trading

The Companies Act 1985 includes the criminal offence of fraudulent trading. This offence is committed by a person who is knowingly a party to the carrying on of business with the intent to defraud creditors of the company.

The Insolvency Act 1986 contains a civil offence, also for fraudulent trading, which imposes a personal liability to contribute to a company's assets on conviction to the court by a liquidator in the process of winding up a company.

general meeting

A formal meeting of the company's shareholders at which the business of the shareholders is conducted by voting on resolutions.

guarantee

A guarantee is a promise by a guarantor to make good any failure by another to meet financial obligations owed to a third person. A guarantee cannot be enforced by legal proceedings unless there is a written memorandum of it signed by the guarantor.

insider dealing	Insider dealing is the term used to describe the use of insider information by any individual in order to make a profit or avoid a loss on a share transaction. Insider information is unpublished confidential information which, if published, would affect the price of the company's shares or debentures.
insolvency	Insolvency is the inability to pay debts as they become due.
liquidation	This is the process by which a company is wound up and its assets realised for distribution to its creditors and shareholders.
loan	Legislation does not provide a definition of a loan. The definition put forward by the courts, and used until legislation states otherwise, is taken from the Shorter English Dictionary which states, that, 'a loan is a sum of money lent for a time to be returned in money or money's worth.' Thus for a transaction to be treated as a loan, there must be an intention that the amount will be repaid.
Memorandum of Association	The Memorandum of Association is a constitutional document of the company which defines the company's powers, objects and relationship with the outside world.
non-executive director	A non-executive director is one who is invited onto the board to assist with policy and strategy decisions, but who does not work full-time for the company. The law makes no distinction between executive and non-executive directors.

ordinary resolution   An ordinary resolution will be passed if a simple majority of the shareholders voting vote in favour of it.

Ordinary resolutions can be used for all decisions at shareholders' general meetings, except for specific resolutions indicated by the Companies Acts or the company's own Memorandum and Articles of Association, which require special or extraordinary resolutions.

parent company   A parent company is any company which has subsidiary undertakings. Parent companies are required, subject to certain exemptions, to prepare consolidated accounts for any subsidiary undertakings which exist at its accounting year end.

private limited company   A company that is not a public company and whose name is followed by the word 'limited'.

prospectus   A document detailing the nature and object of a share issue which invites the public to subscribe to the issue.

public limited company   A company may register as a public limited company (plc) if it satisfies the Companies Act 1985 requirements for so doing eg it must have a minimum authorised share capital of £50,000.

quasi-loan   Quasi-loans are payments or undertakings to pay amounts on behalf of a director by the company with the director subsequently reimbursing the company. A typical example of this type of loan is the use of company credit cards for personal expenditure by a director.

Registrar of Companies The official responsible for receiving and making available for public inspection annual accounts and other information submitted by companies in compliance with the Companies Acts. The Registrar is also responsible for receiving and approving applications for incorporation of new companies.

relevant amount The relevant amount of a transaction or arrangement is the total of all existing transactions or arrangements of a particular type entered into with a director and connected persons.

The relevant amount aggregates the following:

- the value of the proposed transaction or arrangement;
- the value of any existing permitted indirect arrangement of the same type;
- the value of any previous permitted transaction of the same type less any amount paid.

In aggregating amounts, illegal transactions should not be included.

relevant company A relevant company is defined as being any company which is:

- a public company; or
- a member of a group which contains a public company.

shadow director A shadow director is a person in accordance with whose directions or instructions the directors of the company are accustomed to act.

share options   A right, confirmed by agreement, to buy or sell shares in the company.

special resolution   The Companies Act 1985 requires 75 per cent of those voting to vote in favour of a special resolution. Shareholders must be given twenty-one days notice of the general meeting.

Special resolutions are required by the Companies Acts in the following circumstances:

- to alter the company's objects, Articles or name;
- for reduction of share capital;
- for the company to be wound up by the court.

The company's Articles may require any matter to be dealt with by special resolution.

subsidiaries   For the purposes of group accounts an undertaking should be treated as a subsidiary undertaking in any of the five circumstances outlined below:

- where the parent undertaking holds a majority of the voting rights in the undertaking;
- where the parent undertaking is a member of the undertaking and has the right to appoint or remove directors holding a majority of the voting rights at meetings of the board of directors;
- where the parent undertaking is a member of the undertaking and controls alone, pursuant to an agreement

with other shareholders, a majority of the voting rights in the undertaking;

- where the parent has the right to exercise a dominant influence over the undertaking by virtue of:
  a) provision in the subsidiary under-taking's Memorandum or Arti-cles; or
  b) control contract.
- where the parent undertaking has a participating interest in an undertak-ing and;
  a) actually exercises a dominant influence over it; or
  b) the parent and the subsidiary undertaking are managed on a unified basis.

voluntary arrangement A voluntary arrangement is where the directors make a proposal to the creditors with regard to a scheme of arrangement eg to reduce their claims. All creditors are entitled to vote on the proposed scheme. However, any changes in the rights of secured or preferential creditors cannot be approved without their separate agreement.

wrongful trading Wrongful trading relates to situations where a company has gone into insolvent liquidation and at some time before the commencement of the winding up the directors knew or ought to have con-cluded that there was no reasonable pros-pect of the company avoiding liquidation.

Selected further reading

Barc, S, Bowen, N and Braune, J (1991) *Tolley's Company Law*
Tolley, London

Boyle, A and Sykes, R (1991) *Gore-Brown on Companies*
Jordans, London

Crystal, M and Phillips, M (1990) *Butterworths Insolvency Law
Handbook* Butterworths, London

Saunders, G and Smailes, D (1991) *Tolley's Income Tax
1991–92* Tolley, London

Saunders, G and Dolton, A (1991) *Tolley's Corporation Tax
1991–92* Tolley, London

Walton, R and Hunter, M (1989) *Kerr on Receivers and
Administrators* Sweet & Maxwell, London

Whittaker, J and Roney, A (1992) *Directors' Duties and
Responsibilities In the European Community* Kogan Page,
London

Guides to Boardroom Practice (annual publication) Institute of
Directors, London

Guidelines for Directors 1991 Institute of Directors, London

Wright, D and Creighton, B (1991) *Rights and Duties of
Directors* Butterworths, London

Casson Beckman

Casson Beckman is the UK member firm and European co-ordinating office of Summit International Associates Inc. With 25 partners and over 200 staff, Casson Beckman ranks among the top accountancy practices in the UK, and the firm's clients range from private individuals to quoted companies.

United Kingdom office

Hobson House
155 Gower Street
London
WC1E 6BJ
Tel: 071-387 2888
Fax: 071-388 0600

International offices

Summit International Associates Inc is a worldwide association of leading accountancy firms, with over 200 offices in the following countries:

Argentina	Hong Kong	New Zealand
Australia	Hungary	Norway
Austria	India	Portugal
Belgium	Indonesia	Qatar
Bermuda	Ireland	
Brazil	Israel	Singapore
Canada	Italy	South Africa
Channel Islands	Japan	Spain
China	Korea	Sweden
Cyprus	Luxembourg	Switzerland
Denmark	Malaysia	Taiwan
Finland	Malta	United Arab Emirates
France	Mexico	United Kingdom
Germany	The Netherlands	United States
Greece		

Range of services

Audit
- Specialist and business audits
- Statutory audit

Contact: Geoff Barnes

Company secretarial
- New companies
- Registered offices
- Statutory records/annual returns

Contact: Ron Shashoua

Computer consultancy
- System selection
- System implementation
- Project management
- System review

Contact: Ron Shashoua

Computerised accounting
- Financial records
- Management accounts
- Payroll
- VAT returns

Contact: Richard Lampert

Corporate finance
- Mergers, acquisitions and disposals
- Business plans/strategic reviews
- Corporate recovery
- Raising finance
- Flotations and BES issues
- Investigations and due diligence
- Litigation support and forensic accountancy
- Management buy-outs

Contact: Marc Voulters

European & International
- Doing business overseas
- Access to network of accounting firms throughout the world

Contact: Peter Catto or Mary Carroll

Personal financial planning
- Financial strategy
- Inheritance tax
- Partnership tax
- Trust management

Contact: Ian Simms

Financial services
- General insurance
- Independent financial advice
- Insurance broking
- Mortgages
- Pension schemes
- Personal pensions

Contact: Ludwig Haskins

Research and technical
- Information resource
- Library
- Market research
- Quality control and technical support

Contact: Paul Ginman

Tax consultancy
- Compliance
- Corporate reconstructions
- Forensic (enquiry and litigation support)
- PAYE and VAT monitoring
- Planning and mitigation (UK and international)

Contact: John Tipping

Corporate recovery/insolvency
- Corporate restructuring
- Creditors representation at meetings
- Financial and debt monitoring
- Liquidation, receivership and bankruptcy
- Pre-insolvency investigations
- Technical insolvency advice
- Viability studies

Contact: Ian Holland

Current publications

The Casson Beckman Corporate Brochure
The Casson Beckman Financial Review
The Companies Act 1989
Dispute Resolution & Litigation Support
Guide to the Finance Act
Guide to Independent Taxation of Husbands & Wives
Services to the Entertainment Industry
Tax Investigations